Loving Conversations:
How to Pray and Hear God's Voice

DAWN SIMMONS

DEDICATION

I want to dedicate this to the women who let me speak into their lives when I didn't even realize what the Lord was creating in me. The faith and trust you all had in the Lord was the beginning of a ripple that has now affected so many. Thank you for allowing me to be a part of your journey.

Acknowledgements

I want to thank and acknowledge my husband, his patience and support for the last several years as we have followed the Lord's plan. I want to thank my mother who has always been faithful to edit all of my projects and Erica, who was the first one to learn SALO and has never looked back.

Table of Contents

LOVING CONVERSATIONS

1

My Journey Into SALO

I have known the Lord all of my life. As a young girl, I remember singing the songs in Sunday school, working in little paper workbooks and hearing all about Him. At 5 or 6 years old, my grandfather sat me on his knee and transferred Godly wisdom and knowledge to me that, at the time, I did not even remotely understand, but years later flashed into my mind at the exact moment I needed it and has never left my heart. I was saved and baptized at 13, by a very large and somewhat scary German preacher in Stuttgart, Germany. I never strayed too far from the Lord as I entered adulthood. I'm a staying within the line's kind of gal. My late 20's and early 30's were filled with marriage and child rearing. My mid 30's and 40's were growth years.   While I did have a good career, my relationship with the Lord grew exponentially in ways I did not know were still possible in today's modern world. He spoke to me and shared His heart with me, and I was the strongest and closer to Him than I had ever been. However, as I neared 50, I just wasn't hearing from the Lord in the same way I had for almost 20 years. In my mind, nothing had changed. I was reading the Bible, leading Bible studies, going to church, praying and trusting in the Lord, but the silence was unmistakable.

My answer, at the time, to breaking this silence was foolproof. I will fast. I will fast, not for a day or even 2 days or even 3 days, no I will fast in a way the Lord cannot help but to notice. I will complete a 21-day Daniel fast. Yes, this was definitely the answer. Whatever it is that is creating this blockage for me to hear from the Lord will have no chance against a 21-day Daniel Fast. If you aren't familiar with this Fast, it's modeled after the events described in the book of Daniel in the Bible and consists of a plant-based diet. This fast might not seem like a challenge, but for me, I might as well have been standing at the bottom of Mt. Everest looking up. Maybe that's an exaggeration, but just go with me that it was a big deal for me. My logic was simple. Breakthrough happens when you fast, and I needed breakthrough, and I needed it now.

I have come that they may have life and have it to the full

John 10:10

As I prepared for the fast, I laid out my plan. I like plans and I like lists, so I was already excited just preparing in the knowledge that change was coming. I bought a new journal to document the entire event, the good, the bad, and ultimately the breakthroughs would all be documented for me to go back and review and re-experience later. I have journaled for years as a way to hear from the Lord so I wanted to be prepared for the outpouring that will surely happen in the coming days. I had 5 major areas in my life that I was seeking breakthrough. I wanted as a result to see answered prayers, blessings, favor, an outpouring in all 5 of those areas. I not only wanted it, I needed it. I had to hear what the Lord had for me, where was He, why was I struggling to hear from Him. My heart and my mind felt desperate.

I did my grocery shopping for the first week. I was very disciplined for that hour and a half in the store. I did not get anything with sugar, no breads, no pasta, I focused on vegetables and fruit. I have very few, ok, maybe no vegetables I can say I love, but there are some I do like a lot. Of course, those are prepped with bacon or some other fat that is not a part of this fast, so I was trying to develop my creativity, awaken my inner chef that I let take a few years off since the kids have grown and for the most part out of the house. Once home, I got out my containers and got everything lined up on the counter. I spent what felt like hours prepping all my veggies and fruit, trying to convince myself I was going to enjoy this change. I wanted to move forward, and this seemed like a small price to pay.

I also shored myself up mentally for the next 21 days of water. I decided to leave out tea or coffee and stick with water only knowing headaches were inevitable while going through a caffeine detox. I strongly dislike drinking water. I know people who can tell the difference in waters, brands, what mountain the waters came from, and are happy to pay a high price for their favorite water but that is not a part of who I am. The mental struggle I put myself through just thinking about drinking only water for 21 days was a little on the ridiculous side. At that time, my deepest love in a beverage was sweet tea. A love affair that admittedly still exists.

I also pulled together some books on prayer. I leaned on the works of one of the prayer greats, E.M. Bounds. I figured I might need some help with prayer and E.M. Bounds seemed like the right fit. I wanted into that "secret place" E.M. Bounds was known for and I wasn't going to stop until I got inside. Nothing was going to stop me now. I was prepped and ready to go and it all came down to one thing, the date, when would this move of my life begin. The date I chose was September 8, 2018. I want to say a "date which will live in infamy", but it wasn't quite that dramatic. I love history so forgive me now for any excessive use of historical references, it's just the way my mind thinks and tends to keep me entertained.

On September 8, 2018, I started Day One quoting E.M. Bounds in my journal. Somehow putting his words to a few pages made me feel accomplished, it was documented proof I had begun the fast after all. The depth of E.M. Bounds words were somehow magnified as I worked through the morning trying to keep my mind off not only food, but the long 21 days ahead. On page four I began to write to the Lord, write my heart out to Him about why I began this fast. I told him that it started out as needing breakthrough in one area but had grown and had also become about feeling lost. I wrote of how I wanted to get back to Him and His plan. I explained that somewhere along the way, what started out as a journey with Him no longer felt like we were walking together. Then I quieted myself and prepared to wait on His response. What I didn't realize in that moment was that my feeling lost, my not hearing from Him and no longer feeling like we were walking together was all *me*. It had nothing to do with Him at all.

When He spoke, it was beyond comforting. His voice sang in my heart, "Daughter, I am here. I have been and never left your side". From there He began to tell me how he loved me and all that He was doing in me. Over the next three days He had quite a bit to say to me. The one thing you need to be prepared for when you ask the Lord a question is His response. So many people want to hear the Lord, are desperate to even, but you have to go into it willing to listen to him and take to heart what He is saying. Of all the things that people may say to you in your lifetime, through their own filters, hearing from the Lord is different. Hearing from the Lord is the complete and utter loving, encouraging and naked truth. He will never hide behind His words; He cannot do so. He cannot hide behind anything; it is not in his character. He can only speak truth, so when He speaks to you, it's important to listen and understand what He is telling you. There is nothing so sweet as the loving words of the Lord. Even in correction, He is loving and only seeks to guide you or redirect your focus.

For me, the first 3 days were the most important part of the fast. Those were the days I struggled the most to hear Him because I was fighting the headaches, the hunger, I was in physical pain in my body. If you have ever fasted, you know the levels of discomfort I am describing. You are most irritable and least focused in the first few days and yet in that, those days were my best in terms of reconnecting to my relationship with the Lord. Now at this point I will let you know...I did not finish the 21 days. I made it thru day 16. In rereading my journal, apparently pasta was a real craving. I also discussed with the Lord my desire to eat healthier once the fast ended, but I had a pretty good argument for why tacos shouldn't be excluded from my healthier eating regimen. That I will still agree is a truth.

You may be asking what does my fast have to do with you? Let me explain, during the fast the Lord was speaking of many things, He was starting something new in me. He was steering me and clarifying His plan for me and also laying out what He required of me. I asked for a breakthrough, and I got so much more than I could ever imagine. The plan He laid out involved focus, consistency, patience, discernment, understanding, knowledge, faith, trust, and above all, life, life with Him, through Him and for Him. I had a lot of work to do within myself, but He told me there was a long plan for me. He told me that He needed me to hear His voice above the noise, cut through the noise and chaos and pursue Him like I once did. He asked me what I was willing to do. Would I walk with Him and hear His voice regularly? He told me I needed to open my heart. He let me know His eyes were focused on me, but I was not focused on Him. I had absolutely no idea where He was taking me, but I knew I wanted to go there, I wanted to go there with Him. The rest of what I have to share with you is the process He walked me through to develop my relationship with Him and have security in His plan and purpose for my life. I can tell you that the experiences He has brought into my life have been what I dreamed of as a little girl and let go of as a disappointed adult. I let myself become disillusioned by the ugly of the world instead of focusing on the truth and joy of knowing Him for who He truly is in my life and in the world. My hope is that you will take the steps I took, follow what He gave me so you too can have all that He plans for you in your life. He tells us in John 10:10, He came here for us; He came here to give us a full and abundant life. The only way to have that, is to be in relationship with Him and hear His voice for you through the chaos of the world. It takes time, sacrifice, and devotion. Are you willing?

Daniel 1:8-15

But Daniel resolved not to defile himself with the royal food and wine, and he asked the chief official for permission not to defile himself this way. [9] Now God had caused the official to show favor and compassion to Daniel, [10] but the official told Daniel, "I am afraid of my lord the king, who has assigned your[c] food and drink. Why should he see you looking worse than the other young men your age? The king would then have my head because of you."

[11] Daniel then said to the guard whom the chief official had appointed over Daniel, Hananiah, Mishael and Azariah, [12] "Please test your servants for ten days: Give us nothing but vegetables to eat and water to drink. [13] Then compare our appearance with that of the young men who eat the royal food, and treat your servants in accordance with what you see." [14] So he agreed to this and tested them for ten days.

2

Getting Into Position

If you are still with me, then I hope that means you are willing to take the next step toward a full life with Him. So, let's look at what that will involve. The process the Lord gave me is called **SALO**. It's an acronym for **S**top, **A**sk, **L**isten, **O**bey. It took me over a year to fully embrace and execute how to get into position to be in a continual state of **SALO** with the Lord. Since then, I have worked one on one with individuals on how to **SALO**. It is a simple process, but it takes time and discipline, so it is also a difficult process. The elements that will aid you in success are what we are going to discuss before we even breakdown the **SALO** process. Simply put, you cannot skip this preparation work or **SALO** will not happen.

I am going to lay out for you what preparation looks like and it's likely not new information to you, at least I hope it's not if you are already a believer. If you are not already a believer, then this will be more of a struggle and I hope it brings you to a place to become a believer and accept Jesus as your savior. Now where this preparation differs, is how we need to combine it all together and the key to it all coming together for you is consistency. The three elements we will discuss are reading the bible, prayer time and journaling. First, we will discuss each element and understand its significance. Even if you think you know what I am going to say, stay with me and hear me out. Second, we will talk about consistency. We will get real about consistency. You cannot fake it and get through **SALO**. The Lord knows and He will let you know when you are missing something, because truly you are missing out on His best for you. Lastly, we will talk about moving forward in **SALO** and what that looks like for you. I generally like to know where I am going. I rarely, if ever, get in the car and not know where I am going. I mean, a few times I will get in the car to go get dinner and I may not know where I feel like going, but ultimately, I know I am going to get dinner. Likewise, I want you to know where you are going. I want you to be ready to fully engage with **SALO**. It will change your life, it will change your outlook, it will change your outcome. It doesn't just touch you; it touches anyone around you that the Lord wants you to touch. It is the most amazing state of being with the Lord that you will experience. Your relationship with Him will be so close and real you will think you can reach out and feel Him. This, my friend, is not an exaggeration. I may talk about Mt Everest and who knows what else as we go through this together but know that this experience will bring you to your knees, lift you to exuberance, break your heart for those around you and show you love like you have never experienced. You will begin to understand elements around you to move forward with confidence. You will know which direction to go when you have a decision. You will know how to handle any situation in life and know in an instant what He has to say on a matter. This is how I live. This is how we all should live, if we want to do all the things we need to do to get there. If you are not in a place to be honest with yourself, then this is not the book for you, and I wish you the best until you are ready, and I hope you return to go through this process. To live in **SALO** is life changing. All that said, I have now given you a taste of what is to come for you, so let's begin the preparation to get there.

I love love love books. I easily read 20-30 in a year. My favorite book is the Bible. I have bibles in all sizes, font sizes, colors, different translations and formats. My most favorite of all my bibles is one of the simplest. It's a Giant Print King James Version with burgundy bonded leather. By appearances sake, it doesn't look like anything particularly unique or special, but to me it is one of my most prized possessions. If I lost everything, it would be the one thing I would want to save and the one thing I would grieve for if I lost. It belonged to my grandfather. Through his influence I know Jesus. He raised my mother and all his 7 children to know Jesus and when he passed away, that was what I wanted of everything he owned. I believe it was his most prized possession. As I write this today, I received a new bible a few days ago and I have another one on the way. Yes, I do actually read them all. They are all different. My archaeology bibles are where I spend most of my time. I love the historical aspects that come to life as I read. So, for me, reading the Bible is a part of my life. It is time blocked on my calendar. There are a lot of ways out there to read the Bible, there are apps and audio books and reading programs designed to help you read, but the bottom line no matter what you chose to do is you have to read, and you have to read consistently. Now I will say that to read and to not understand or not be engaged in what you read is not what I am talking about. If you are not understanding what you are reading, then you need to find a study Bible that does make sense to you. Apart from that issue, reading the Bible is done for multiple purposes. The first is for you to know the true character and nature of God. This is critical in the **SALO** process. Reading the Bible will build you in your Bible knowledge, it will filter into your heart. It provides examples and references you can use in your life.

It is alive and will speak to you and bring more life into your life. The Bible is your compass. This is my continual message on my YouTube Channel, Life Journey with Dawn Simmons, where I urge people to open up their Bible as we travel the world discussing biblical topics. Reading and knowing the Bible is the framework of your relationship with the Lord. You can't know Him if you do not know the Word, they are the same. If you do not have a reading plan, find one that will work for you. Find one you can do consistently, and consistently means daily or multiple times during the week on a set schedule. It doesn't matter if you know the Bible by heart, still read. This is not a race by the way. Read at a moderate pace so that you are growing in the Word as you read. There is no value in reading quickly just to say you finished whatever amount or creating a reading plan that moves so quickly you aren't experiencing the Word. That is not our purpose and it will not help you in **SALO**. Once you have a reading plan in place that will work for your schedule, commit to it. A huge challenge I see for people trying to live in **SALO** is their Bible reading drops off or never fully got off the ground. Be honest about what you are putting into this process. If you spend the proper time in this area it will help you to decipher between His voice and your own in **SALO**. We will go into this deeper as we discuss the Listen step, but I cannot stress enough that you cannot decipher and know Him without reading the Word.

For the LORD gives wisdom; from his mouth come knowledge and understanding. He holds success in store for the upright, he is a shield to those whose walk is blameless

Proverbs 2:6-7

Once you have put your reading plan in to practice, then move on to focus on prayer time. My mother is an intercessor, I am not. Intercessors can happily spend hours focused in prayer, I cannot. We need intercessors, but they cannot do it all. That is not their role. We are each responsible for our own prayer time and we want to develop that aspect of our life. Prayer does not need to follow a formula. Jesus gave us a great formula for prayer, but He does not intend for every prayer to follow a formula. He wants us to pray from the heart. When I am meeting one on one with someone on **SALO**, I will ask them to open our session in prayer. Many times, my request is met with reluctance because no matter who you are, praying out loud can be uncomfortable. People get caught up in the eloquence of their words and not the content of their heart. In **SALO**, prayer is essential because it opens the line of communication between your heart and the Lord. You do not need anyone to run interference for you, you can go straight to Jesus. To prepare for prayer in **SALO,** you will need to pray, and you will need to pray from the heart, not once a day, or twice a day, but in a prayerful mode all day. That does not mean you need to be praying/talking (mumbling, closed off somewhere) all day. We can't function if we are praying/talking all day and we have work, kids or other areas we need to have our attention directed towards. The purpose is to move away from praying only when we need something or when something bad happens to a place of having the Lord right there with you all day long available at a moment's notice. When you live in **SALO**, that is your prayer life. Commit to consistently be in a prayerful mode all day and you will quickly see the intimacy develop in your relationship with the Lord. Consistency in this area will open larger doors for future communication. Sadly, according to a Pew Research study released 12/14/21, only 45% of American adults pray daily. This is down from 58% in 2007. If we could be consistent and show others how valuable prayer is, we could make a difference in the lives of everyone around us.

Devote yourselves to prayer, being watchful and thankful.

Colossians 4:2

The third element we need in place for **SALO** is journaling. Now even if you don't like writing hear me out on this. When the Lord begins to speak to you, you need to write it down. You will not remember what He is telling you. When He wants to have a conversation with you, it could be several paragraphs or even several pages. You want to have a historical record of what He said and on what date. One of the things you will be doing is going back to reread what He said to you and I guarantee over time you will see patterns and specific direction given to where and how He is guiding you. He will have already given you an answer, multiple times but you still have not followed through on what He said, all while still asking Him for an answer to that very same question. Sounds unbelievable, but I have yet to see someone go through this **SALO** process and not have some aha or oh yeah moments when they realize He has been speaking to them and answering them all along. No one is above it because **SALO** takes time to develop at each stage. When you hear from Him, you will regret it if you did not take the time to write it down. So, save yourself some heartache now and pick up a journal.

When you journal, I encourage you again to date your entry and start off sharing your heart with the Lord. Tell Him what is on your mind. Give Him your thankful heart. Give him praise. Develop those aspects of your relationship with Him. From there, write about a scripture or a struggle, but let it be from the heart. This journal is not intended for anyone but you and the Lord so don't hold back. Be transparent with Him because He already knows, and this is an exercise more about you at this point than Him. I want you to get comfortable writing to Him, even if you think you are not a good writer, that does not matter here. Your heart is what matters and I want you to develop a flow. You have your own writing style and it's important to get comfortable in your style, so it doesn't distract you when you are in **SALO**. When I work with people who are not used to journaling, they struggle at first to free themselves and just write. Grammar and punctuation are not important (sorry to all my English teachers out there, but it is a sacrifice we need to make here). For the writers out there, don't try to be too flowy or poetic, this is not the time for that either. Just be you. Write like you speak and it will be easier. My ask of you is this: start a consistent journaling schedule just like you have done with reading the Bible and prayer time.

Once you have all three elements working together equally, this is what it should look like:

SALO ACTIVITIES

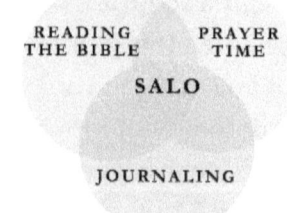

READING
THE BIBLE

PRAYER
TIME

SALO

JOURNALING

Our objective is to consistently be in that center triangle when we are in **SALO**.

Let's go over a little about consistency and the important role it plays in **SALO**. In order to consistently stay in that little triangle requires discipline. There are no shortcuts here. Figure out your schedule and stick with it. I don't say this to discourage, I actually say this to encourage. When I hear someone struggling in **SALO**, it is highly likely that at least one of these three elements is not happening. That said, life happens, and when we don't have a plan for those moments, we lose our consistency. We have vacations, family visits, we get sick, an unexpected death, holidays, extra heavy workload, I could go on and on here about how life happens that alters our plans. Be mindful of when this occurs because what I have seen happen is one week turns into two weeks and wonderful momentum you may have had will be lost as you reposition yourself to get back to **SALO**. It may be subtle at first, but the longer you are away from your bible, prayer and journaling the harder it is to get back. Maintain discipline so these times are either short lived or find a way to incorporate your activities into your short-term situation. These are times when the Lord may have a lot to say to you and wants to have a conversation with you to comfort you or give you new ideas to be more efficient. One of the women I work with was struggling with her work schedule and the Lord gave her a complete plan on how to structure her day and it made a huge difference not only for her work life and personal life but her journaling time as well. He cares about everything in our lives. If you hear nothing else in these last few minutes, hear this; consistency is crucial to success in **SALO**.

Finally, what will **SALO** look like for you. If you are looking for your purpose in life and you want to know what the Lord has planned for you, you can find His answer in **SALO**. If you have major decisions in your life, you can get His direction in **SALO**. If you want to know the Lord's heart in a matter, you can ask Him and hear that and so much more in **SALO**. If you are sitting in a meeting and need to handle a situation right on the spot, **SALO** will provide His answer.

SALO takes honesty, consistency and discipline. Are you willing?

The LORD is near to all who call on him, to all who call on him in truth.

Psalm 145:18

LOVING CONVERSATIONS

3

(S) STOP

Traditionally, when a person prays, there is a need or they are trying to decide what to do, but it isn't their first course of action. By the time prayer begins, time has already been spent thinking about the need, maybe analyzing, worrying, coming up with options, thinking about consequences or just outright taking action and, as a result, there may be some unexpected consequences that further complicate a situation. Today in particular, people seek quick responses. Decisiveness in our culture is seen as a sign of strength, and I am guilty of thinking that as well. When someone can make a decision and move forward, I typically like that in a work environment because we can move forward faster. Everything in our lives now moves faster and at a quick pace. We can cook our food quickly, get information quickly, travel relatively quickly, have items delivered quickly, you name it, we can likely do almost everything in our lives quickly if that is our intention. We rarely take time to truly **S**top and think before we act. The unfortunate result is we often miss out of the Lord's best for us by doing that.

Before the Lord introduced me to **SALO**, I made plenty of decisions on my own. Unfortunately, they were not all good decisions, and I am a decently intelligent person with common sense. I would think things out and look at an issue from multiple angles, so I felt at the time I was making an informed decision. What I didn't know was how much I could not see, but the Lord knew. In December of 2019 my husband and I were thinking of purchasing a local specialty food business. I managed a place like this when I was younger, the location was good for us given that is was near my other business, we could afford to buy it and we had some strong ideas to build it up in to more than it currently offered. I knew of good people I could trust for labor, and I had a good relationship with the owner of the building who was all for us buying it. I should also add the business had a good profit margin and was profitable, so we were starting from a good place. There didn't seem to be any reasons not to move forward aside from the added responsibilities I would have overseeing 2 businesses. On the outside, it wouldn't seem like this was a decision I would need to go to the Lord about because there wasn't a conflict or a concern or any red flags. It seemed like this was one we could handle on our own and move forward. We did, however, decide that since this was a major decision, that we should

Stop and ask the Lord about it before we do anything. So, my husband and I each went to the Lord and to our surprise the answer was no. It was so surprising in fact, that I thought maybe we misunderstood. I brought it up to the Lord a second time and what I discovered was a no the first time has the exact same meaning as a no the second time. So, we did not move forward, and it was ultimately purchased by someone else that same month. Although we were slightly disappointed, I let go of the thoughts of what could have been and moved on in life. That simple step of Stop and the follow through on **SALO** saved us thousands of dollars in expenses as the world shut down only a few months later and my state remained shut down for a good portion of 2020. We obviously had no idea, no way of knowing what was to come, but the Lord did, and He spoke to us and guided us away from a financial burden we would have faced.

As you read this, you may think, okay, I can Stop before I make a decision, it's not that complicated. It may not be complicated, but it is hard. This act, to Stop, before we move forward is probably one of the harder parts of **SALO**. This act requires our mind to change. This act requires our heart to be directed and aligned with the Lord. This act requires the strength of commitment. There is a learning curve and once you feel like you are completing the **S**top when you should, you realize all the moments that got away and you should have taken a moment to **S**top before you moved forward.

Come near to God and he will come near to you.

James 4:8

Let's look at how many people internalize the decision-making process when they don't know what they should do. I have found working with individuals through **SALO** and initially in my own life as I was learning **SALO**, is that it is harder to yield to the Lord in situations where you are facing a major life decision. The yielding feels like a loss of control.   A loss of control produces more fear even though most of us can readily admit that when we don't know what to do we aren't actually in control at all. These are situations where there may be a lot at stake and the wrong decision could be harmful to you or someone else, expensive if you are wrong or difficult to get out of if you change your mind. I call this situation being in a Silo Cycle. In business, operating in a silo isolates a group or department and can interfere with communication, efficiency and produce less favorable outcomes. In our lives, we enter the Silo cycle on our own and we come around and start again, on our own. There is no real progress in the Silo Cycle. It produces frustration, confusion, anxiety, a feeling of being overwhelmed. It creates in you a feeling of uncertainty. I see people over and over get stuck in this cycle unable to progress to answered prayer and guidance from the Lord.

Let's take a look at what this looks like in the following illustration.

SILO CYCLE

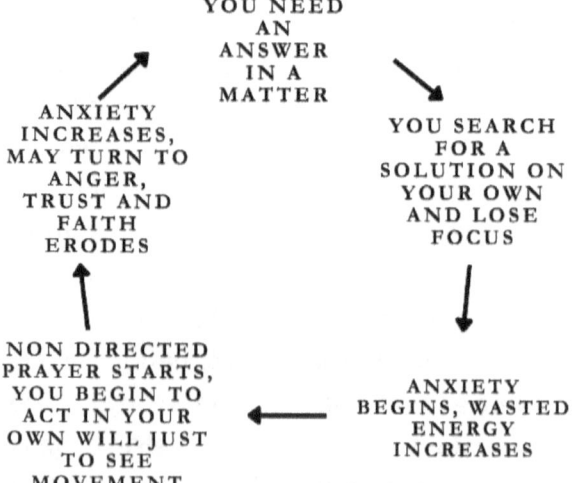

YOU NEED AN ANSWER IN A MATTER

YOU SEARCH FOR A SOLUTION ON YOUR OWN AND LOSE FOCUS

ANXIETY INCREASES, MAY TURN TO ANGER, TRUST AND FAITH ERODES

NON DIRECTED PRAYER STARTS, YOU BEGIN TO ACT IN YOUR OWN WILL JUST TO SEE MOVEMENT

ANXIETY BEGINS, WASTED ENERGY INCREASES

We start off needing an answer regarding a specific matter. Most of us are familiar with this situation. We have a problem, or a choice and we just don't know what we should do. You begin trying to search for solutions. Spending time searching often leads to losing focus in other areas of your life including your relationship with the Lord. The search may have yielded more information you have to sift through that may not be helpful in your situation. Anxiety begins to increase and your wasted energy increases as you try to decide what to do. You begin to pray to God for guidance, but you also begin to act in your own will for a solution just so you can feel like you are moving forward. Your anxiety continues to increase because you don't see a resolution. Anxiety may turn to anger as trust and faith in the Lord erodes because you don't think He is providing a response. You have now come full circle because you still need an answer in a matter. The cycle continues.

One of the bigger challenges I have found in working with people through the Stop process is they are used to handling major decisions using a Silo Cycle, but they don't recognize they are in the Silo Cycle. From their perspective, they prayed about it and didn't get an answer to prayer. It's what is normal to them. What the Lord has shown me is that, in reality, the Lord is rarely the first-place believers turn to for guidance, but rather one of the last. Time and time again I have seen that He is right. Often, we don't turn to Him in prayer until after a mess has been created instead of ahead of time to understand His plan and path for our lives. It doesn't matter how educated you are, how much money you have, how old you are, how much experience you have, we all have a Silo Cycle at some point in our lives. I want to help you get out of yours and into the Lord's plan for you in relationship and decision making with Him. In order to do that, I want you to look at decision making with **SALO**.

SALO PROCESS

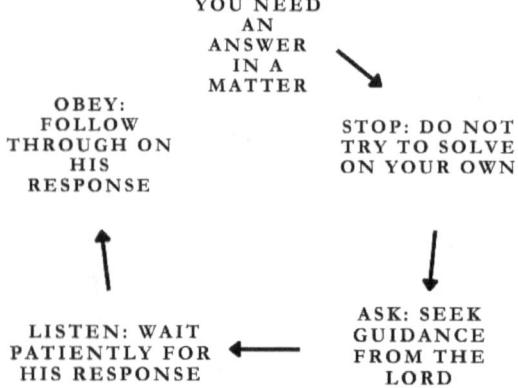

YOU NEED AN ANSWER IN A MATTER

STOP: DO NOT TRY TO SOLVE ON YOUR OWN

ASK: SEEK GUIDANCE FROM THE LORD

LISTEN: WAIT PATIENTLY FOR HIS RESPONSE

OBEY: FOLLOW THROUGH ON HIS RESPONSE

We start at the same place, but that is the only similarity.

We start off in need of an answer regarding a specific matter. Before we do anything, we

Stop:

Recognize we need to be in alignment with the Lord, **S**top acting on our own and commit to follow through seeking Him

Then we

Ask:

We seek the Lord for His plan for us and **A**sk the Lord in our journal for His plan for us

Now we

Listen:

We wait patiently for His response and write it in our journal

And then we can

Obey:

We trust the Lord in His response and we follow through and **O**bey His guidance and direction

Now that you have a better idea where we are going, let's get back to the Stop process. As I've stated above, it is difficult because it is new, it is change and how we currently behave are our habits or our unique traits. What I am asking of you is to step into the unknown, but I am asking you to take the step toward the Lord so it shouldn't be a fearful step. These first steps are the biggest steps you will ever take if you follow through with **SALO**.

One of the women I work with one on one was very consistent in **SALO**. She had progressed well in her prayer time and her journaling dramatically improved over the course of six months. She tried different times, different locations to be able to find what fit her schedule. She changed as a woman and her relationship with the Lord grew exponentially. She would **SALO** over all sorts of situations and I didn't think she really needed me to work with her on the process any longer until she got some devastating news regarding one of her siblings. What I want you to understand here is you can feel like you have mastered **SALO,** but when something comes at you that is devastating, or can have a tremendous emotional impact, you can easily revert back to Silo Cycle behavior. A traumatic event can trigger an emotional response that can be difficult to recover from or regain focus from to put your eyes back on the Lord. I have seen people crumble and lose their way and not even resemble themselves. I had a woman come to me who I had not seen in about 6 months. She is a beautiful woman, always perfectly dressed and professional. Unfortunately, she was experiencing emotional trauma surrounding a job loss as a single mom. When she walked in the door, I did not recognize her. Her physical countenance and her mental and emotional countenance had taken such a beating that she was no longer herself. The Lord never leaves us in times like this. Let me share How the Lord worked in both women's lives.

Call to me and I will answer you and tell you great and unsearchable things you do not know.

Jeremiah 33:3

The first woman, let's call her Esther, was feeling disconnected after she received the devastating news. She spent months praying protection over the situation and was struggling to fully understand what happened and what was true and what was not true. One of the beautiful benefits of a journal is being able to go backwards and reflect. As we discussed her situation, one thing became apparent, we needed to take a moment and just **Stop**. We needed to **Stop** to regain composure and to regain focus. I asked her to clear her mind and go back to **SALO** and ask the Lord for the truth in the situation. One of the wonderful things about the Lord is He will reveal truth, but He will only reveal what we need to know. Sometimes we don't need details, we just need to know the basics and what He wants from us in that situation. A second thing I directed her to do was to go back through her journal and reread what the Lord revealed to her when she would pray and ask about the situation. Afterward she realized that the Lord had spoken to her months ahead of time to prepare her for what was coming, but she had forgotten about those journal entries. Taking that time to **Stop** and refocus so she could go back to **SALO** was crucial for her to understand the Lord's plan in the situation. He had a plan all along.

The second woman, let's call her Ruth, was having some self-worth issues. Her prior work environment was very toxic which took its toll, but then she lost her job on top of it all and it was devastating for her. I hadn't talked to her about **SALO** prior, but I put the building blocks in place for her to begin immediately. Thankfully, she stepped forward and started praying, journaling, reading the Bible and then hearing from the Lord. Within about 4 weeks of our meeting, she had another job, closer to home and it paid well. Her relationship with the Lord was stronger and she could hear him and felt his love and encouragement. If you are willing to **S**top where you are and submit to the Lord before you move forward you give Him the ability to alter your outcome and guide you to what He has planned for you.

What I don't want for you is for a negative situation to be the reason you are in a place where you are willing to **S**top and seek the Lord. My hope is that you are reading this wanting and desiring a closer relationship with the Lord regardless of what is happening in your life. What I want for you is for you to have started your preparation work from the previous chapter. What I hope is that you will take your prayerful mode as you see situations arising in your life and change your reaction, which leads us to the steps of **S**top.

The first step is to *recognize* those areas in your life where the Lord should have input. For me it is money, my marriage, my business, how I run my household, it is pretty much every area where I want his best for my life. When I began, I started out with only the big areas of money, business and my marriage. As I began to see shifts in these areas, blessings, favor and growth, I began to commit more areas to the **SALO** process with the Lord. Remember, it's not always about what the Lord is going to do but can also be about the Lord keeping you out of things that are not what is best for you. We don't always know why at the time, but if we trust in Him, we don't need to know why.

In all your ways submit to him, and he will make your paths straight.

Proverbs 3:6

The second step of Stop is to *slow down and come to a complete Stop* in reacting and decision making. It takes time to get into the habit of slowing down and stopping yourself from moving forward. It may even feel uncomfortable. It's just like when you are driving your car and you are approaching a stop sign. You gradually slow down and come to a complete stop before you enter an intersection. In the slow down process, you come to a complete **S**top and you do not move forward with any action. Just as at a stop sign, you wait and make sure you are clear to move forward, the **SALO** process positions you to know from Him not only if it is safe, but which is the best way you should go. Essentially what you are doing is telling the Lord you are willing to submit to Him so you can be in alignment with Him and receive His best for your life before you move forward. If you go into it understanding that is the purpose, it is easier to integrate and develop the habit of **S**top. This is difficult because it must be a conscious effort to change. So many of the things we do are without thought and therefore without a full understanding of the plan the Lord has for us.

The third step is to *commit* to the Lord that you will follow through with seeking His input. It is easy to say you will do it, but you need to commit to taking the time and taking the commitment seriously. You can't pick and choose when you want to commit and when you don't. Also, do not commit to anything you know you are not willing to do. We aren't talking about a making commitment halfheartedly. We are talking about a commitment to the God of the Universe so say what you mean and mean what you say. I see this step overlooked most frequently amid an emotionally charged issue.   It can be very frustrating because we overlook it and then wonder why nothing is happening. We will go more into depth as we progress through **SALO** but understand now that without this commitment you are more likely to be in the Silo Cycle and not make it through **SALO**.

Commit to the LORD whatever you do, and he will establish your plans.

Proverbs 16:3

Remember that there is a learning curve, and it will become apparent as we progress through **SALO**. It may be easier for you to start by focusing on a specific topic but do not chose a topic that is emotionally charged. For example, if you are having marital issues, I would not recommend you choose that as your topic. I want you to use the topic you chose while you learn **SALO** and I don't want you to make emotionally charged decisions while you are learning. Once you are committed and have your topic chosen, let's move forward and begin to **A**sk.

*But blessed is the one who trusts in the L*ORD*,*
whose confidence is in him.

Jeremiah 17:7

4

(A)ASK

I want to take a minute and recap where we need to be before we move into the **A**sk process. By this point your reading time, prayer time and journaling should be firmly in place and consistent. You should be familiar with the **SALO** process and have a good understanding what you need to do in the **S**top process and have chosen at least one topic you want to start with to **SALO**. Are you ready to move forward?

The first point I want to address in **A**sk is our starting point. We must be aligned with the Lord. Let me show you what I mean by aligned. In the illustration below The Father, Son and Holy Spirit are the beginning, the top, our source, our focus, our Comforter, our very life. The creator of the Universe and everything in it. We know that what we ask of and receive from the Lord will yield the best for our lives. There is no question about this because it is the character of God that He is our provider, our refuge. Through His blood we have Life. The Holy Spirit is our Helper, our Light in the darkness. All things holy and true come from our Father, His Son and the Holy Spirit. Reading the Bible confirms this and explains to us the nature of God and the abundant life we can have in Him. In John 15:5, Jesus tells us *"I am the vine; you are the branches. If you remain in me and I in you, you will bear much fruit; apart from me, you can do nothing."* Because we know this, we want our hearts, our minds and our bodies aligned with our Father, His Son and the Holy Spirit.

FATHER,
SON & HOLY
SPIRIT

ME

JOB, HOME,
FAMILY,
DECISIONS,
MONEY,
VOLUNTEER
ETC

Moving down you will see an arrow, to represent the relationship we have in Him. The communication we can have to ask and pray and seek from Him or as we read in **Matthew** 7, to ask, seek, and knock is not only expected of us but desired by the Lord himself. He further tells us that if we do ask, seek and knock, we will receive, find and the door will be opened to us. This arrow represents that two-way relationship. As I prepared myself in understanding **SALO**, the Lord described several issues on his heart for you and me. As we move forward in **SALO**, from here on out we are going to be discussing what the Lord revealed to me to in my own life but also what is on His heart for His people. It is not all puppies and rainbows. God is a God of Love, but He is also Truth and that means that He does have to share with us details at times that are not beautiful, but are meant to give us an understanding, knowledge and encouragement to move forward to His plan and purpose for our life in Him.

The arrow pointing down from "me" represents the priority we need to have for everything else in our lives. Nothing should come above our relationship with the Lord. I often hear people say that their spouse or their children are their first priority and then God. Particularly in blended families, of which I am one, you will hear spouses say the children from their previous marriage have priority over their new spouse and that is not biblically correct. In Matthew 6:33, Jesus tells us *"But seek first the kingdom of God and his righteousness, and all these things will be added unto you."* This is Jesus telling us how to position our heart. If that doesn't convince you then how about when God speaks these words to Moses in Exodus 20:3, *"You shall have no other gods before me."*   Now I can already hear someone out there arguing that placing children before God is not the same as placing a god before Him. You can argue that point all you want, but it doesn't make any sense to argue that with anyone, ask the Lord yourself. Go to Him and hear what He has to say about putting anything before your relationship with Him. You will not be able to fulfill God's purpose and plan in your life if your relationship with Him is not first. If you go into a second marriage putting the children first, and your new spouse and God second, you are setting your children up for another divorce. There is stability in having Him as your first priority. He will be the One to guide you and help you navigate all the challenges a blended family can bring. According to CompareCamp, the U.S. divorce rate in 2020 for first marriages is 42%, down from 50% in the 1980's. This could be that fewer couples are choosing to marry and are instead living together. However, the staggering truth is the divorce rate for second marriages is 60% and third marriages a whopping 73%. Hear me when I tell you that putting Him first in your life is the way to the abundant life He came here to provide for us, it is one of His promises to us. If He makes a promise, it can be nothing other than the Truth.

As I said before, this alignment has to be our starting point in **SALO**, but it also has to be our position in Him evermore. We cannot start out aligned and have good intentions and then over time slide back to old habits. This alignment is where we as believers need to be always in our relationship with the Lord. If we remain aligned with the Lord, our intentions, motivations and desires can be focused correctly on Him, and over time our **A**sk becomes less about us and more about Him. The Lord revealed a few things to me about alignment. He talked about His desire for His people. He truly wants us to **A**sk. He urged me, *"Ask Me. Ask Me throughout your day"*. As I began to develop the process of **A**sk, I wanted to do it in a way that was faithful and true and honoring to the Lord. I focused on making sure I was in alignment with Him and one day His response to me left me overjoyed, *"You continually ask for My Hand in all you do. I will honor your requests. You will know My will."* Hearing this, I knew I was correctly focused on Him and wanted to go deeper and hear more of anything He was willing to share with me.

I did decide to be careful in how I prepared my **A**sk because I knew I was developing something new with Him. At the time, I did not know that **SALO** was being created for me to share with as many people as possible. As I continued further with Him, I knew that while I did get specifics for me, this was not about me. This process is about you, this is about helping His people know Him better. He continually encouraged me with His words " *Search Me out. Find Me to hear Me and then you will know that I am always available to you. Always open for questions and will always provide answers."* Hearing that, I would go deeper and **A**sk more questions. There were days I needed to know more about which direction He wanted me to go and He would provide powerful encouragement that would help me to grow where He needed me to grow. One of the ways I would ask is by leaving my questions open. For example, I had a day when I was questioning myself and I prepared my **A**sk, I wrote, Lord, what do you have to say to me on this. He responded to me *"Pray and have faith. Your faith at times is a mustard seed, but I need it to grow and be consistent. You cannot always be a mustard seed."* That response was extremely important to me because it let me know that I needed to build my faith. So I spent time focusing on building faith while developing an understanding of why I had a lack of faith. I cherish those moments. When you can hear from the One who knew you before you were formed, on how to grow and truly become what you were designed to be, you get excited and want to give this gift to everyone around you who will listen. Whenever I would **A**sk, He responded. Some days it was simple *"Pursue Me. Pray. Keep your petition moving."* Other days, when I needed more lifting, He would always provide *" I am with you. I walk with you daily. I hear your heart. I know your frustrations. I see it all. Your voice is familiar to me as mine is to you."*

Over time, as I began to understand the plan the Lord had for me, I never took for granted the gift He was giving me in our communication. He was faithful to give me reassurance when I felt the enemy interfering *"My word is your key. My word is your covering."* The more frequently we spoke, the longer we spoke. Understand "spoke" here means journaling. I was careful to always write our conversations so I could review what He shared with me. At times He shared pages and pages of information with me that I would never have remembered on my own. I knew His heart for me. I understood His trust in me when He shared with me *"You never ask for anything I cannot and will not do."* This was very humbling to hear, and I appreciated that He would share that with me. Above all else, I wanted to never take advantage or fail to show the level of respect that was always in my heart for Him. I took nothing He gave me lightly and at times when He showed me His heart for His people, I could feel the pain I know He feels for those who do not know Him. There are believers who know of Him, but do not truly <u>know</u> Him. A relationship has not been developed and because of that He shared *"I want more of My people seeking more of Me. Most live only a fraction of what I have for them. Unrealized outpourings."* That saddened me for you on your behalf. I knew I was in a place where I would receive His outpourings, but to think of you out there missing out on His best for you, while you struggle or function in less than what He can provide for you. The thought that you don't have a relationship with Him that will easily provide you with His wisdom and guidance for your life, just broke my heart for you. He did also talk to me about others. Those who claim to know Him, but as He described *"Be aware of those aligning for themselves. They are not truly seeking Me. Those who genuinely seek Me, want Me, that is enough. Out of that comes a desire to be like Me and glorify Me."* While this saddens me and I am not fully in position to help someone who does not want help or who will not listen to me, what it does provide is guidance for us. The Lord saying this further exemplifies my point that you cannot fake it in

SALO. The Lord knows our hearts, our motivations and our desires. We cannot hide in our hearts anything from the Lord. He knows, He loves us anyway, and does want us to turn to Him, but in order to do that we must be honest with ourselves and Him. From there, He can work in our hearts.

If you want the best answer, we need to ask with the best intention

I've shared with you how we **A**sk and what can come out of our **A**sk, but I want to give you steps to follow to get you positioned to **A**sk. First, we need to be aligned with the Lord. Our hearts, our minds, our bodies need to have Him as our first priority. James 4:3 tells us the importance of our hearts *"when you ask, you do not receive, because you ask with wrong motives, that you may spend what you get on your pleasures."* Second, we need to have an idea of what it is we want to **A**sk, and we want to be specific at times. For example, if you have two job options, talk to the Lord about each one and **A**sk Him which one is His plan for you. The reason I recommend this, especially if you are starting out, is this is more definitive and when you ask more definitive questions you will get more definitive and precise responses. If we ask questions so wild open that we don't know where we are even going with our own question, we are unclear if what we are hearing in response touches on what we were trying to ask about. We then begin to question the credibility of what we hear. Our God is a God of order, so when we approach Him, it is better to approach Him with some order to our **A**sk. As you progress you can be more open, which leads me to my third point. If I don't have a specific need for a given day, I will simply **A**sk, Lord, what do you have to say to me today. It is an open-ended question, but I put the parameters on it giving Him the freedom to talk to me about anything He chooses for that specific day. What I don't do is limit Him. I don't try to box Him into any specific response or test Him to try to try to get the answer I want to hear. You can certainly **A**sk for a confirmation, which we will talk about later, but I never test Him or try to manipulate an outcome.

If you haven't been journaling regularly before you begin the **A**sk process, this will be more difficult for you. When I explained that I wanted you to get a flow, it was to help you discern between your own writing and His response. It is crucial you have prepared yourself in this way before you begin. So you want to take your writing from the heart to Him and begin to present your thoughtful Ask of Him.

This is the confidence we have in approaching God: that if we ask anything according to his will, he hears us.

1 John 5:14

5

(L) LISTEN

Up to this point, everything we have discussed has required discipline, a lot of discipline. Ideally you have retrained yourself to be living in a life designed for **SALO**. If you are being honest with yourself, then I suspect you can admit it has not been easy to get to this point. There are moments of easy, sure, but overall to keep yourself positioned and to be disciplined about the time you are investing and the change in behavior that has and will continue to come with this **SALO** process is not easy. It takes time and focused energy to be disciplined and maintain consistency. Those skills you have developed were not by accident. Far from it. Without those skills to support you, you would not be able to move forward into the next step which I find to be the single most difficult to master and that is to **L**isten for the Lord's response.

We have done the work to be aligned with Him, and we need to stay aligned. We have changed behavior to slow down and **S**top before we move forward with a decision in our own power and strength. We have developed our frame of mind and heart to be able to **A**SK the Lord for his guidance over our life. All of this while continuing to read the Bible, pray and journal consistently.

We have had to forego other activities, get up earlier, adjust our daily work schedule, reevaluate our priorities and even eliminate a few things along the way that would have impeded our ability to continue through the **SALO** process. I want to acknowledge this because this alone has developed your relationship with the Lord to be stronger than I suspect you ever anticipated. If that's all this were about then that would be good, right, we are in a better relationship with the Lord than we were. We, however, are not here for good, we are here for great and as Paul encourages us in Philippians 3:14, *"we must press on towards the prize*, the prize for us here of Listening to the Lord respond to us individually. He has a personal message, a plan and a purpose for each of us and He is waiting on us to be able to hear Him, to listen to what He wants to tell us and give us abundant life. After all you have done, are you willing to step forward and dig in deeper to hear His voice? If the answer is yes, then let's not waste another minute and get going.

Earlier I said that I believe Listen is the most difficult to master of the entire **SALO** process. Why would I say that? Well, everyone I have mentored through **SALO** and even including myself as the Lord walked me though the **SALO** process has had moments, and I mean multiple, several, many moments where they question themselves as they Listen. Doubt, fear, self-confidence issues, uncertainty all rear their ugly heads in Listen. It is an unavoidable part of moving forward, but it can be easy to address. Another factor that makes this the most difficult is a lack of patience as we are waiting on the Lord's response. Finally, if we have not been faithful in the journaling process or our Bible reading that becomes very evident in Listen. So let's tackle each one of these in reverse order.

We will start with the importance of being faithful in journaling and reading the Bible. Recall from the Getting Into Position chapter that there were several reasons I gave for the importance of journaling and this is where those reasons play out. Your own unique journaling style is very important to develop in speaking to the Lord. It needs to be as much a part of you as how you talk to people. You need to establish and develop your voice, who you are and how you sound even to yourself. You should recognize you in your writing. It sounds silly, but it is crucial to supporting you as you begin to hear from the Lord. We will go into this in more depth shortly, but I wanted to bring it up as a reminder of why we are doing the activities we are doing in **SALO**. Secondly, reading the Bible has not only brought you closer to the Lord, but it has given you more perspective on His character and His heart not only for His people that we read about in the Bible, but for you as well. The point I am making here is that you will know Him by His Word once you begin hearing from Him. As you Listen for the Lord, His response will align with who He is in the Word, who you know Him to be because of the time you have spent reading the Bible. If you hear anything not in alignment with His word, then you are not hearing from Him. So this ties in to the point I raised previously about Doubt creeping in as you Listen. Let's talk about Doubt, fear, self-confidence issues and how all of those breed uncertainties. I can tell you without hesitation, with zero degree of uncertainty that those emotions are not of the Lord. There is one place that those emotions are derived from and that is the enemy. We are human and I understand how easy it can be to allow those emotions to creep into your journaling time, but do not allow it. The moment you allow those emotions to enter your heart and mind, you have allowed the enemy a seat at your journaling table and he has no place there. Coming into agreement with the enemy allows him access, gives him rights, spiritual legal rights to be there and participate in what you are doing. This is not an area to take lightheartedly. This is a time for battle if this happens to you. I don't want to say it will, I don't want to speak prophetically in any way over you for that, but it happens so easily we don't always recognize it when it happens and I want you prepared, I want you to be on guard to address it head on in that moment. This principle is crucial, not just for **SALO**, but in your everyday life. The answer is so simple. The battle can be won so easily. The moment you see any of those emotions coming at you, REBUKE IT in the name of JESUS!!! Luke 10:19 reveals to us

Jesus' words on the subject *"I have given you authority to trample on snakes and scorpions and to overcome all the power of the enemy; nothing will harm you."* Need a little more convincing? How about Isaiah 54:17 *"No weapon formed against me shall prosper"*. The Bible is filled with words that reveal to us our power and authority over the enemy because of the blood of Jesus. The enemy knows it, if you have any doubt, refer to Paul in Romans 14:11 referencing the Old Testament *"It is written, As surely as I live; says the Lord, "every knee will bow before me; every tongue will acknowledge God"* That is not just referring to us humans, we were here last, think about who was here first and before us. This is a Biblical truth that if you do nothing else from reading this book, take that with you and apply it.

If any of that is new to you, please take a moment to absorb that. New to you or not, you need to address it in your mind and heart so you are prepared and ready should it come up. Up to this point we have not needed to address the spiritual aspect of this process but understand **SALO** is spiritual and if your heart is not open to it or your mind is closed off to it, then you are not allowing the Lord a way to reach you. He will try to change your heart if you ask, but ultimately it is up to you to make that decision. Our God has given us free will, you have to choose to take it or not and the irony is that if you do not, then you are actually losing your freedom, not gaining it. We are only free in Him and that is what allows us access to Him.

So let's move onto the final factor I see that can get in the way in Listen. Patience is one of the Fruits of the Spirit but some of us are fruitier than others. I happen to have a little less fruit in this area. My husband most kindly pointed it out to me one day (not that I didn't know it) when I was agitated, and I made the comment many of us have said "that (insert frustration here) is on my last nerve!" His response "oh, is that the one next to your first one" Admittedly, I found this hilarious in the moment, but I did not laugh, I commended him for his humor and I did allow it to diffuse my mood, but to this day it is one of his most memorable and hilarious truths about me. I actually have yet to mentor anyone in **SALO** with less patience than I have, and I still see patience as a huge factor to overcome. Are you asking why is that? Well, most of us are conditioned that when we ask a question, especially in this situation where we have done so much work to get to the point of even asking a question, that we want a relatively speedy response. In **SALO**, there's no guarantee of that. In **SALO**, He may have our answer ready for us but maybe we aren't ready for the answer. There are a multitude of reasons why we may need to wait, and He may choose not to tell us, we just need to wait. Instead, He may give us the answer we actually need, but we are so focused or consumed even, with what we want to hear, that we don't hear what we need to hear. Sounds totally ridiculous, doesn't it? You would think, if the God of the Universe, the Ancient One, The Great I Am, the one who died on the cross for us, if He spoke, we would not only hear it but we would Listen to what He has to say and you know what, we don't. There are people you may have heard of that have heard the audible voice of God, there's no mistaking it. That's not what I am talking about here. Those are usually one-time occurrences over a particular situation and those are wonderful, I hope that happens for you if you want it, but that's not **SALO**. In **SALO**, this is an everyday event where we are in conversation with Him. He does not use a loud commanding baritone voice that brings us to our knees. He can, but that's not His purpose here. His purpose here is a Loving Conversation. Yep, we finally get to the point of the title of this book. Our time with the Lord in **SALO** when we Listen and He responds we are in loving conversations!!! He is bringing to us love, encouragement, confidence, understanding, revelation, knowledge, wisdom, joy, peace, patience (a lot of patience) and sweet kindness. Yes, at times He will discipline us as He guides us but He does it lovingly so we know it is for our best interest. The purpose of our time with Him is to build that relationship, to hear His plans and purpose for our life, to move into that abundant life He promised and in that time with Him, we become more like Him. The more time we spend with Him in these conversations, the easier it gets. The more you experience with Him, the more you want the people around you to experience Him, and the people you don't even know to experience Him. That's why I am here, to share this with you, so that you can have all that He promised us and gave His life for us to have with Him and for Him.

So, now that all of that is out of the way, deep sigh, how do we Listen? Well let's backtrack a minute and walk through this together. We have been diligent to this point and we have our question that we want to ask all ready to go. For the first few times at least, I would find a place to journal where you can have privacy, no interruptions and are able to focus for the next hour. This means seated comfortably, make sure your pen is fully functional and you are completely emotionally and mentally available and in good spirits. At this point I would get my worship music started and go ahead and open our journal and date it. I recommended worship music strongly in the Getting Into Position chapter to help create the atmosphere. I want you to be comfortable with the music, so it is not a distraction at this point because our journaling changes, it shifts from this point forward. We are pressing into the Lord, and we want to create the atmosphere that is inviting the Holy Spirit to join us, and it also helps prepare your heart and mind to come together to receive from Him. Begin your prayer over your journaling time and start writing from the heart as you usually do.

Here are the steps to journaling:

First:
Start with your praise of who He is: this can also act as a defense for you over your time because the enemy cannot withstand an atmosphere of praise for the Lord

Second:
Thanksgiving: Share what you are thankful for in your life or the lives of your family

Third:
Repentance: Remember to seek forgiveness for anything you may have done to grieve the Holy Spirit this week. We don't want anything in the way of coming to the Lord with a clean heart. This is similar to the concept of preparing ourselves for communion as discussed in 1 Corinthians 11:28. "Everyone ought to examine themselves before they eat of the bread and drink of the cup"

Fourth:
Present your Ask (specific request)

Fifth:
Listen for His response (after I have presented my Ask, I turn it over to the Lord by saying "What do you have to say today Lord". That clearly delineates

that I am done speaking and will prevent me from rambling and it serves as my invitation for Him to speak. It's a way of saying, the floor is yours and I back up to let him take over. I also am specifying that I am only seeking what He has for me today knowing that He will share with me as much as He decides, but clarifying my expectation is not for Him to lay out the entire plan and purpose for my life in one sitting. It could happen, but when we go back later to review it helps to keep things in perspective for us, particularly during the Obey process.

How are you doing so far? Are you ready to move forward? Ok, let's talk about how to Listen.

Once you have written, "What do you have to say to say, Lord", or however you chose to word it, now you wait. You wait without your own thought or intention. Now don't try to focus too hard here. I liken this period to those 3D images that became popular in the 80's or 90's where you see an image in an image. If you over focus you actually lose focus because you are so focused on being focused that all you think about is being focused. This is always an area I need to coach people through because it feels awkward to sit in silence and wait in a time where we have our phones occupy any moment of downtime or boredom. We need to go back to a simpler time during this and just enjoy the peace and quiet our minds to just wait.

For some people they need a little help so here is a list of ways to wait without losing yourself in the wait:

> Try to sing something simple that you can do without thinking

> Repeat Jesus over and over slowly

> Let yourself lightly flow into the worship music in the background

> Say "Thank you, Jesus" over and over slowly

> Close your eyes and sit in silence

What will happen as you Listen, very lightly you will hear a prompting in your heart and your mind. You will hear a response letting you know He is there. At that point, your pen should be writing. You want to record exactly what is being said to you. The first few times it may be short. Do not be discouraged by that. One of the women I work with was entering into Listen for her first time and she heard Him speak to her with one sentence. She came back to me and sounded disappointed because she only got one sentence. In her defense, she knew that I receive pages and so she had an expectation that she too would have pages her first time, but that's not how it works. I had to point out that on her first try she received a response from the Creator of the universe, and it was an entire sentence, not a single word or a fragment of a sentence (inferring she actually heard the entire sentence, which is a great thing). He wanted to share with her, and she heard it! That should be celebrated. When we do this, do not compare yourself to others. We are all different. So when you are doing this, maybe you won't even receive the very first time, that's ok. It means you need more opportunity to Listen for Him. It does not mean that He wasn't there, it just means you need to try again and reexamine if there was anything you need to change to allow you to Listen more easily. Don't give up and do not be discouraged. Can we go back a minute to the first thing I told you about this step: it is the most difficult to master. It will happen if you have put all the steps into practice, He will be there. I guarantee He will be there because *"He is Faithful and True"* Revelation 19:11. My ask of you is this, you have come this far and you came this far for a reason so keep at it and remember what Paul tells us in Romans 8:25, *"If we hope for what we do not yet have, we wait for it patiently."*

Once you have heard from the Lord, Listen does not end there. This is the time when we need to evaluate what we received. When you were writing you should have written down exactly what you heard exactly when you heard it. Do not change a single word, all words matter. When I am working one on one with someone in **SALO**, after they have Listened and written down what the Lord had to say we come back together to evaluate and discuss the experience. Inevitably, this is where I will be asked "How do I know this is from Him and not me?" If the person I am working with hasn't experienced doubt or the other emotions up to this point, we want to be careful how we address this question as to not invite that as an option now. So I will ask them to describe the experience to me, where were they, were they distracted, how easy was it to focus, just so I can understand where they were in that moment. If everything is presented as positive, then we move on to how they felt when they were Listening to what the Lord had to say. When the Lord speaks, it should come at you at a comfortable pace (He knows this is new to you and that you are writing) You should feel a peace in those moments and the words themselves should be presented in a loving positive affirming way. The content of the message should be in alignment with His character or His Word. If you receive something long, it's not likely you will remember it verbatim, parts of it maybe, but it should be something you need to go back to review because if it is coming from Him you won't remember it the way you would as if you were forming the thoughts. If the message leads you away from your relationship with Him in any way, then it is not from Him. The enemy will want to draw you away, the Lord will bring you closer to His heart and His hand over you. Also, we need to understand that His response is not always what we want to hear. If everything you ask gives you a response of exactly what you want to hear, you may need to look at your process and where you are not allowing Him to truly intercede and respond to you.

The more you do this, the less you will need to evaluate because you will know when it is Him and when you have lost focus and are interjecting yourself. If at any point while you are writing you feel an inkling that you are projecting yourself, stop. Do not continue writing. Pray and go back through and start again rebuking anything, including yourself from interfering with Listening to the Lord. That can happen at any point, no matter how experienced or spiritually mature you are. We are still human, and we need to be mindful that we make mistakes and just redirect and do it again.

Once you have a good grip on this, mastering takes months to years depending on the time you invest, but once you feel solid that you are able to Listen to the Lord when He speaks then move on to Obey. Don't move too quickly because Obey takes the longest to master. It's not the hardest, but it takes the longest. Before you embarked on this journey with me, I told you **SALO** was a simple process but because it takes time and discipline it was also a difficult process. You have pushed through the difficult so far and we have just a little more to go. Once you make it through Obey, you will have the outcomes I promised you from the beginning, but way more importantly than that you will have the abundant life and the outcomes Jesus has promised us throughout the Bible. So let's stop wasting time and get on to Obey.

Listening Reveals Clarity and Creates Calm

6

(O) OBEY

Before we begin **O**bey, can we stop to take a moment to celebrate here. You have to this point put in some serious hours and if you are at this point, then you have put in some heart, possibly some tears and had some moments of rejoicing. That is no small thing, and we need to acknowledge that about ourselves. The people around you may have no idea the changes you have made or are making, but the Lord does. The Lord has been watching you this whole time, cheering you on, at times when you didn't even know it. He has encouraged you and prompted you to continue and move forward to meet Him where He can give you more and develop you into who you were created to be in Him. Take a minute to reflect on the you at the time you started this and the you now and give Him your praise and thanksgiving for all that He provided for you to get to this point right here, right now.

In this **SALO** process, we have developed some habits to assist us in **O**bey. Primarily this involves our journaling but a part of it involves how we have grown our relationship with him to be developed by His responses in **L**isten. Let's walk through **O**bey and then we can discuss the challenges and why I said earlier that it takes the longest to master.

For **O**bey our journal becomes our most valuable possession. Our journal possesses the words we have received from the Lord and if lost, we could never recreate. In addition, there are days where you have shared with the Lord some deep emotions or maybe you have some issues you are working through with His guidance. Our journals are meant to be personal to us. So, I am always mindful of where my journal is and am never careless with it.

One of the things I asked you to do when you journal is date it. This is important because part of **O**bey is to review our journal entries on a regular basis. It's very easy to receive from the Lord, be excited about what He had to share, feel relieved about a situation, and then move on and forget the little detail of following through on what He asked us to do. I made this mistake and every single person I have worked with has made this mistake. Especially when you receive multiple pages or are receiving pages every day. His requests get lost in all the other information He shares. From the outside looking in, you would think I am exaggerating this point, but it is rather astonishing how easy it is to fall into this trap.

But the plans of the Lord stand firm forever, the purposes of his heart through all generations.

Psalm 33:11.

So know now that failure to follow through is normal, but what I am hoping to do here is help you to become abnormal. Being normal is not always a good thing and in this circumstance, it's actually harmful. To illustrate my point, I want to share with you what the Lord has discussed with me on how to obey him. There are 3 categories we are going to discuss because those will be the same three categories you will encounter as you begin the **O**bey process.

Focus: Unless you are someone that can be so hyper focused that nothing can interfere or distract your thoughts when you are working on something, then the Lord will give you words to encourage, corral, correct or whatever means necessary to bring you back to where He needs to be. The first time you hear this feels a little odd, but I am appreciative of it now because He is quick to let me know if I am distracted and not on point with what He needs from me. We are human, so it happens and it is why I tried to encourage you to start journaling in a focused manner. You know your habits so prepare appropriately, but know He will redirect you as well.

Guidance: When you have positioned your Ask and have Listened and taken His words, then you will know His words in response offer you guidance. The thing is, we are quick to take His guidance, close our journal and move on to the next day and we didn't actually go in the direction He asked of us. Instead, we will forget what He told us and come back the next day and Ask the same question again. One would think that if we Asked a question we sincerely needed an answer to and received one, we would jump into action and use that guidance right away. Incredibly, we forget. Incredibly, we still focus on the question we Asked as if we did not even receive a response. Now hear me on this, we can be so focused on our question and whatever turmoil surrounds it that we let that feeling linger on weeks and months. We have hundreds, if not thousands, of interactions, conversations, tasks, projects, responsibilities and opportunities in our modern lives everyday that we simply overlook details. We don't just overlook them however, we don't absorb and let the Lord's words, His guidance sink into our hearts and minds.

Follow Through: Once you have received His guidance, He gives us time to complete the follow through on His response. Whether He gave you very detailed instructions or a general pointing in the direction you should go, He gives us time to move forward in His plan for us. As I stated before, when we don't do that, He will come back to you and ask for your follow through, to **O**bey Him. Another way He has spoken to me in this area is to give me encouragement as a reminder for what He has spoken previously. This can be helpful if you have received a word from Him and then something happens you weren't expecting. I will give examples of this shortly. I will also share with you examples of how He will use follow though as a way to shore us up and reinforce a point He has made earlier when we encounter a trial.

Over time, He will use other categories in developing your relationship with Him, but these are the first ones and each person will experience Him in ways specific to you. Just be open and willing and He will meet you exactly where you are.

As I begin to share my personal examples, I want to be very clear about the importance of **O**bey.

Focus and Follow through develops discipline and eliminates chaos.

As the Lord worked with me to develop the **SALO** process, He had to have a lot of patience with me. Understand that I knew He was doing something new in me and with me but at the time I had no idea it was something for you also. I wonder sometimes, had I known, would I have been a little quicker to pick up what He was trying to instill in me. I was very focused on what I was working on and trying to accomplish and so I assumed all His remarks were strictly intended for me. For the most part they were but a structure was being created. Now that said, I do want to reiterate that **SALO** is for you. It's to create a process for you to develop your relationship with the Lord to enable you to hear Him on His plan and purpose for your life. It is not to be used as a weapon against anyone else to get them to do what you would like, to see things your way or to tell someone that God said someone was wrong and they needed to do everything your way because God told you so. If that even enters your mind or you hear someone say that, you need to rebuke it. Don't even take the time to breathe before you rebuke it, that's the accuser at work.

Okay, let's start looking at some examples of what the Lord has said to me. These examples are reflected in the three categories we just discussed, but some are a combination. We will start with looking at Focus, then Guidance, Follow through and lastly examples that are combinations.

Focus

These are examples of what He spoke to me to get my mind back on Him. There are many journal entries where He simply said "Focus" to get me back on track, but these are examples I wanted to share that shows His heart for me. At times, you may have something happen or someone say or do something towards you that is contrary to the truth. You have a natural reaction of being upset or where you let the situation hijack your focus. If you take that to the Lord, He will respond and pull you back towards Him, bring you peace, encouragement and affirm you.

"Remember to keep your eye on Me"

"It's all about Me, remember that I will be your compass"

"Don't lose sight. I am here to guide you"

"Focus on My words for you and My direction to guide you to My opportunities"

"Focus, you cannot hear Me if you are not focused on Me"

Guidance

These examples are specific to me and what I was needing at the time. You can see from His responses that He is guiding me by His character, drawing me closer to Him and building me up to be at peace in His plan and purpose for me.

"Give Me time. Grow in Me"

"..discipline, time and apply the wisdom I have given you. I want you to use it in situations I will be placing you in"

"Prepare yourself for our next steps. Everything becomes important, our time, our direction, our focus, our actions, our prayer time and our strategy. Change is coming and I want you to be able to pivot to handle many things at once and not be overwhelmed."

"My words carry power every day. You want to make sure you are not directing this. I want to make sure you are hearing Me and seeking Me."

"Shift your thinking, your old patterns don't work. We need new ways to accomplish bigger goals."

"Pursue Me. Hear My heart on every matter instead of being overwhelmed by the vastness of what you think you can't do. I will equip you. I will be there with you."

"Pursue Me in all matters"

"Don't tackle more than one issue at a time or that's what it becomes and that's not My way. Order. Order is My way to solutions. Stay consistent with Me in our planning sessions."

"I need you close to Me to understand and know My plan in all circumstances brought to you."

"Don't let disbelief fill My space in you. Don't let doubt and discouragement take hold."

This last one I want to talk about for a minute to explain the context. I was hearing from the Lord daily and I knew what He wanted and asked of me.

I used to host a meeting on a regular basis with believers who were for the most part mature believers. On this particular day in April one of the people there was telling me she was hearing from the Lord about me, over my life to guide me. This was a mature believer so I didn't object to her speaking, but what she was saying was not at all in alignment with what I knew the Lord was doing in my life, and I had an uneasy feeling in my Spirit. I did not receive her words but I did not rebuke them either. The meeting ended and I went to the Lord about it. So the next example is His response to my inquiry.

"All you need is to hear My voice, follow Me when you see Me guide you."

Now I am sharing this with you because if you live in **SALO**, you will likely encounter a situation similar to this. I do believe the Lord gives words of knowledge, which are words from the Lord for someone else that wouldn't otherwise be known but from receiving it from the Lord. There are times the Lord will use people with this gift to share with people that may not hear Him otherwise or may be used to confirm. I have been both the recipient and the giver of words of knowledge so the existence of this gift from the Lord is not up for debate here. Believe it or don't, I know it to be true. My caveat here is that there are people that will claim to have this gift and it is either false or the origin is not from Him. So I am not apt to receive everything someone tells me. If you have no experience with this, understand that there are some rules to these occurrences and whether you receive or rebuke these words given are part of those rules. In this case, this behavior in the group continued and I was ultimately directed by the Lord to rebuke this person's words in the group. Once you are hearing from the Lord yourself, this is less likely to be something you will experience. The reason you are less likely to experience it is because you don't need someone else giving you a word when the Lord communicates with you directly. However, if that does happen, just take it to the Lord and have Him either confirm or deny whatever was said. If ever prompted for a response when a word is given, you can gracefully say, "Thank you, I will ask the Lord about that" and move on without creating a long drawn-out awkward moment. If later that person comes back to you and asks you about the word, be honest if they were not correct. Also, make it clear that you do hear from the Lord consistently. The Lord will direct you how to handle situations, but sometimes if you are caught off guard, I wanted to arm you with a way to be graceful and not receive anything the Lord does not want in your life.

Obey also referred to as His Follow through

These are examples of the Lord reminding me where we are going and what I am to be doing. He is kind in how He brings me back to where He already asked me to be, or affirms I am where He asked me to be and it builds me up in Him.

"Remain steadfast in our time."

"You need to remember our time involves prayer and worship. Find the joy in what we are doing."

"We do have a plan and I need some follow through on your part. Keep building. I want you to gain and grow in endurance. Our journey is not short."

"The things I will ask you to do will not always be easy things. Knowing I can count on you to follow though is important. Not everyone is willing to do the hard things, but My work is not always pleasant."

Combination: Focus, Guidance & Obey (Follow through)

As you read these understand that in a few of these He is correcting me. He already gave me His guidance and I wasn't moving forward in what He was guiding. The more times He has to repeat Himself, the more direct He becomes, but it is still in love and when I receive these type of words, it brings me such encouragement that no matter how many times I wander off, He is there to bring me back to Him.

"Do not focus on what you do not see, that is not your journey. You focus where I direct and I will take care of the rest."

"You have ideas, I need you to execute what I give you and move forward on My breath."

*"Be at peace with Me. I told you yesterday, Be Still. I need to know you hear and **O**bey, follow My voice. Hear Me and take to heart My words."*

"Pull together and streamline your thoughts. I want you thinking of Me and our plans. Do not discount the little things."

I know you can do all things; no purpose of yours can be thwarted

Job 42:2.

I hope these examples bring you encouragement and motivation to dig deep with the Lord in your relationship. I want this encouragement to sustain you and carry you through when you face challenges in **SALO** and particularly challenges in **O**bey. To work through the challenges is going to require action on your part. You need to consistently go back through the words He is giving you and make sure you are **O**beying or following through on what He says. I know I have missed opportunities, and I should not have and would not have had I stayed on track and **O**beyed in what the Lord asked of me when He asked of me. Put on your calendar now when you will go back and review each week to keep from getting too far down the road without review for **O**bedience or follow through. I could be more direct and say lack of follow though is actually the nice way of saying disobedience. No one wants to hear they are being disobedient. We all want to think we are in control of our lives and our outcomes. We don't want to have to answer to anybody and we want to do what we want to do. There was an example from my journal I wanted to share earlier and decided not to, but the Lord is saying to share it with you now.

"My work requires a maturity many are not willing to attain because they love their life as it is and keep Me at a distance."

When He tells me these things, and I hear them frequently as He discusses His heart for His children, I hear His desire for His children to know Him, not the entity He has been made out to be, but the real and true Savior of the earth who, even though He didn't want to, he willingly gave his life in a most painful, brutal and humiliating way so we could live. *"...I came that they may have life, and have it to the full."* John 10:10.

As far as learning **SALO,** I have given you the tools you need to change your life from uncertainty to security in Him by developing a purposeful foundation and relationship with the Lord, enabling you to have Loving Conversations with Him. You now know how to pray and hear God's whisper to you. So what is left, Staying in **SALO**.

7

STAYING IN SALO

The 21-day Daniel fast I started years ago has taken me on a journey with the Lord I never imagined and am thankful for every day. My relationship with Him is my greatest reward. My plan and purpose have been revealed to me over the last 4 years and this book is only one part of it. There are opportunities I missed, I know that, and I wish that were not the case, but I can make sure going forward I am consistently doing my part to fulfill His plan and purpose for me. We all have our part. He never asked us to do everything. Creating "Life Journey with Dawn Simmons" on YouTube and the "Conquering Our Unseen Enemies Podcast" have allowed me to reimagine old dreams and create new dreams and it is entirely because I listened to Him and followed His guidance.

Since you are my rock and my fortress for the sake of your name lead and guide me.

Psalms 31:3

For me to remain consistent in **SALO** for all these years now goes back to the basics and time management or actually priority management. My schedule has **SALO** time on it to make sure I keep it in the forefront of my day. The Lord has been very clear with me as He developed me that His time is important for us to continue to move forward together in His plan. What He is telling me is when I am not moving forward with Him, I am moving forward with my own plan and will ultimately have my own outcomes, not what He designed for me.

Process Produces Changed Outcomes

Now that **you** have entered into the **SALO** process, I hope that you commit to it and find as I have and as Paul so eloquently wrote in Acts 17:28, *"For in Him we live and move and have our being.."* We should be celebrating right now that you have made it to this point and are no longer the same person you were when you started. We should celebrate that if you remain consistent, you will never again be unclear or feel uncertain about what you need to do. When we are consistent and we stay in **SALO**, the outcomes in our life have meaning. I have been fortunate to watch people remain in **SALO** and grow in their relationship with the Lord and find peace over circumstances that previously created turmoil. Family issues, marital struggles, finances, are no longer areas of stress and heartache because of the understanding of His plan. Accepting He does not need or want you to do everything and the Holy Spirit bringing contentment to your spirit are life changing moments.

You have to truly understand that consistency breeds confidence and clarity.

Have confidence in who you are in Him and what you are doing for Him. Have clarity in knowing you are doing what you are doing because He is the one directing you. If you come to a time when you feel you have dropped off and things are not the same when you are hearing from the Lord or you are not hearing Him, I want you to come back, revisit this page first to help get you back on track. If you still need help, go back to the basics. Ultimately, you will need to put the time back in to getting yourself repositioned. Consistency in **SALO** is a commitment not only to Him but to yourself as well.

The one who gets wisdom loves life; the one who cherishes understanding will soon prosper.

Proverbs 19:8

As I close these pages to prepare for you to open them, I want to leave you with this. Honor the Lord with your time. It will be the best investment you ever make. Whenever you have a concern or an uncertainty:

Stop and **A**sk the Lord. Then **L**isten and **O**bey as He directs.

SALO PROCESS

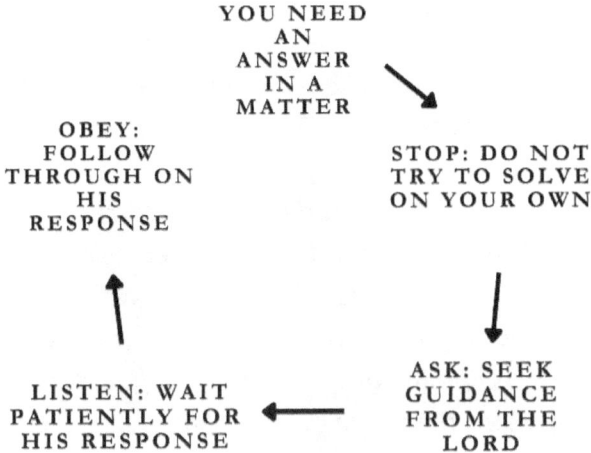

YOU NEED
AN
ANSWER
IN A
MATTER

OBEY:
FOLLOW
THROUGH ON
HIS
RESPONSE

STOP: DO NOT
TRY TO SOLVE
ON YOUR OWN

LISTEN: WAIT
PATIENTLY FOR
HIS RESPONSE

ASK: SEEK
GUIDANCE
FROM THE
LORD

Faithfully follow these steps and stay consistent in your time with Him. As a result, you will always know His plan for you, and you will have security in Him every day of your life.

If you feel you need additional support, then join the SALO Circle Membership group on the Loving Conversations website. The information is listed in the back of the book.

In Jesus' name, Amen.

Luke 6:47-49

As for everyone who comes to me and hears my words and puts them into practice, I will show you what they are like. They are like a man building a house, who dug down deep and laid the foundation on rock. When a flood came, the torrent struck that house but could not shake it, because it was well built. But the one who hears my words and does not put them into practice is like a man who built a house on the ground without a foundation. The moment the torrent struck that house, it collapsed and its destruction was complete."

ABOUT THE AUTHOR

Dawn is an author and speaker on Biblical topics having worked with thousands of individuals across the globe on topics including relationships, marriage and hearing God's voice. She is the host of "Conquering Our Unseen Enemies" Podcast and as a lifelong world traveler, she is the YouTube host of "Life Journey with Dawn Simmons." Over the course of her life, she has visited numerous archaeological and biblical sites which fueled her passion to help individuals understand biblical history and how it relates to our lives today. With education and research in both Business and History, including 20 years of mentoring and teaching, Dawn's coaching methodology helps people to better understand the Bible and develop their relationship with Jesus. Dawn is a mother of 4 and lives with her husband in Ventura County California.

Connect with us!

For more resources on how to develop your relationship with the Lord using the **SALO** method, join the SALO Circle membership community at our website:

www.lovingconversationssalo.com

Contact us at:

contact@lovingconversationssalo.com

Follow us on Instagram:

lovingconversationssalo

Related Title:

Loving Conversations Study Guide and Journal: How to Pray and hear God's Voice

ISBN: 978-1-960775-06-1